Mind Right, Life Right

Manifesting Dreams Through the Laws of the Universe

By Ash'Cash

The Law of Attraction is just a piece of the puzzle.
Find out how you can use the Laws of the Universe
to make your dreams come true

DISCLAIMER

The advice contained in this material might not be suitable for everyone. The author designed the information to present his opinion about the subject matter. The reader must carefully investigate all aspects of any business decision before committing him or herself. The author obtained the information contained herein from sources he believes to be reliable and from his own personal experience, but he neither implies nor intends any guarantee of accuracy. The author is not in the business of giving legal, accounting, or any other type of professional advice. Should the reader need such advice, he or she must seek services from a competent professional. The author particularly disclaims any liability, loss, or risk taken by individuals who directly or indirectly act on the information contained herein. The author believes the advice presented here is sound, but readers cannot hold him responsible for either the actions they take or the risk taken by individuals who directly or indirectly act on the information contained herein.

Published by 1BrickPublishing

A division of Ash Cash Enterprises, LLC

Printed in the United States

Design by Pixel Dijajn Studio

Copyright © 2017 by Ash'Cash

ISBN 978-0983448662

DEDICATION

This book is dedicated to those who are looking to live their best lives by manifesting their dreams and aspirations!

TABLE OF CONTENTS

INTRODUCTION

The Laws of Attraction is Bullsh*t

The Law the attraction is bullsh*t!!! Everyone's always talking about thoughts become things, good vibes only, positive energy, negative energy and when it comes to fulfilling your dreams, people make it seem like if you just wish to the universe all of your dreams will come true! I don't know about you but I am sick and tired of people acting as if the law of attraction is the end all be all to everything you want in life. What about good ol hard work? What about grinding and hustling for what you want? What about persistence? What about resilience? All of the things that I know go into fulfilling your dreams... Ok I know... I went off the handle just a bit, but let me explain...While the law of attraction isn't totally bullsh*t, it's actually just a piece to the puzzle.

It started in 2006 when Rhonda Byrnes came out

with the movie The Secret. In the movie, she simplifies the law of attraction and does a great job of introducing it to the mainstream. There have been many books before that discussed the law of attraction, but this one just did a better job at explaining it in such a way that it was received by more people (Or maybe more people were just ready to receive it). After seeing the movie, then reading the book, I became someone who was fully attached to the concept of thinking something into fruition and for a long time I was able to attract a lot of great opportunities but none of them really stuck. As I started to study more, I was introduced to other Universal laws and realized that the Law of Attraction did not paint the full picture.

Everything requires a process point, blank period! If you want something there WILL be a process that you must undergo to attain it. If you do not follow the full process then there is a slim to none chance of you obtaining your desired results. For example; if you have a craving for lasagna, you **thought** about how delicious it tastes, you **visualized** the robust marinara sauce, the melted mozzarella cheese and the smooth velvety ricotta filling and your mind and your stomach **affirmed** that lasagna is what you want for dinner

-unfortunately that is not enough to make the lasagna magically appear. To add to that, even if it's in front your face you will have to do something in order for you to enjoy the dish... Like eating to feed yourself! Now back to the lasagna ; merely thinking about it will not lead to you fully enjoying the meal. So let's say you decide you want to cook the lasagna your-self. Ok now this will require you to create an action plan first taking stock of what ingredients you have on hand. The next step will require you to go out and buy the ingredients you need, then after following your recipe using precise measurements and layering of the ingredients and then placing it in the oven at the right temperature, for the right amount of time, then and only then will you have your desired results and be able to eat the dish. Even if you decided not to cook the dish and go to a restaurant instead, you would still have to find a restaurant, get dressed to go to the restaurant, travel to the restaurant, order your food at the restaurant and then eat the food at the restaurant. This may sound like I'm being trivial but the truth of the matter is that just thinking about a thing is not go-ing to lead to you enjoying the thing... and when it's all said and done what we really want out of life is to enjoy our thing (which if I stop using the word thing

I merely mean your dreams and aspirations.) That's why I say the Law of Attraction is bullsh*t or the way many have tried to portray it is bullsh*t. Yes attracting what you want is a major part of getting what you want but there is a process that happens prior to attracting it and a process that happens after you attract it. Combine those processes together and that is how you manifest your dreams.

Not too long ago I was one of those people that thought that the law attraction was the end all be all. Let me tell you - I would attract some of the best life-changing opportunities that one can only imagine but they never amounted to anything long-lasting. I would get a taste of the dream but because I didn't know the other laws that governed the universe, a taste was all I was experiencing! I would get annoyed because my reality was not in line with my dreams and aspirations. Do you know how frustrating it is to be right there at your dream but can't really experience it continuously? Well that was my story but now that I understand how the universe works, I use her to get exactly what I want out of life. I have a beautiful family, a career that I love and the privilege to inspire and motivate millions of people every single day. I have an awesome support system of family and friends, I make a good living and as I continue to elevate in this human experience I will continue to use the universe to live in peace and bliss.

Part of that bliss is to be a messenger for those who are ready to receive the message of abundant living and as the Zen proverb says "When the student is ready, the teacher will appear." I believe that we are all put here for a reason and while many people will not realize what the reason is for them within their lifetime, I am fortunate enough to understand that my purpose is to make the world better than how I found it and this is my true intention.

I wrote this book as a guide for those who have the same questions that I had and to share the knowledge that has been imparted to me. My hope is that you will receive this and use it to maximize your full potential. As someone who doesn't believe in coincidences I know that if you have read this far into the book then you are exactly where you belong. The universe doesn't make mistakes, so you reading these words at this time is part of the divine plan!

My message to you is simple: The Universe that we live in is precious beyond our wildest imagination. It contains infinite possibilities. In order for these possibilities to exist, there must be universal laws and principles that bring order to the chaos. Without these laws, life and all of its possibilities would not exist because everything would be based on randomness or accident. Be clear that NOTHING that happens in life is random or by accident. It is ALL happening for our greater good (If that is what we are intending).

Depending on where you look there are many variations of the Universal Laws. Some sources cite as little as seven to as many as one hundred and five. I have studied many of the laws and based on my experiences as well as the experiences of others, for the purpose of manifesting your dreams, this book contains what I call "The Mindset Principles" which are comprised of the laws of the universe and they're designed to bring you peace, happiness and access to all of your desires. For generations these laws have been used by secret societies and royal families to bring them tremendous success, wealth, and power.

Whether or not any of the aforementioned is your aim following the "The Mindset Principles" WILL help you manifest your dreams.

Thoughts do become things! But with the right intentions, actions, allowance, and more, those things will become EXACTLY what you want them to be. Welcome to Mind Right, Life Right: Manifesting Dreams Through the Laws of the Universe!

Let's get started!

PART I

THE MIND AND WHAT PART IT PLAYS IN MANIFESTING DREAMS

Mind Right, Life Right

The Three Types of Minds

Before you can begin using the Mindset Principles to manifest your dreams you must first understand how the mind works and what part it plays in the dream manifestation process. There are three levels of the mind and each level is important and serves its own purpose. The three levels are: the Conscious mind, the Subconscious mind, and the Super Subconscious mind.

The Conscious mind

The Conscious mind is where you get your rationale and logic from and where your thoughts are produced. It's broken down into two parts; ideas and feelings. Right now as you read this book, whatever thoughts or feelings you are having is being produced by your Conscious mind. It is somewhat limited, because it draws its conclusion based only on your observation, experience, and education. What your mind perceives as right or wrong is only based on what you've been taught, so in essence if you were taught the wrong things for all of your life, your Conscious mind is going to believe in those values whole heartedly because it doesn't know otherwise.

The Subconscious mind

The Subconscious mind is where you get your emotions and feelings from and is a representation of who and what you are. It operates on its own and is not biased to what thoughts it lets in. Your Subconscious mind does not operate based on how true or false an idea is, instead it believes that anything that is allowed in is true and gives it life through your feelings. It can be persuaded and when it accepts something as true, it creates logic to coincide with the idea no matter how absurd the Conscious mind may think it is. Have you ever had a great day, then all of a sudden someone tells you some bad news or you see something disturbing on social media and it automatically ruins your day? That feeling is controlled by your subconscious. It has accepted this unpleasant information into your mind and dictates to you how you should feel. Sometimes you don't even realize that it has affected you until later or maybe not at all. If you sit down and think about your mood swings, you will realize that they come from the subconscious with no help or control from you consciously.

Mind Right, Life Right

The Super Subconscious mind

The Super Subconscious mind is where all of your creativity and faith lie. This is where your spirituality and belief in the unknown or unseen is produced. Your Super Subconscious mind is always operating on a subconscious level and has unlimited access to all the ideas feelings and information that is stored in the subconscious. It also has unlimited access to all information outside of your observation, experience and education. This is where you get your intuition and inspiration from or what we call your "gut feeling". It is what motivates you into action and responds to clear commands of ideas and energy. It is the light bulb that lights up in your head "out of nowhere". Your Super Subconscious mind does not respond to time; the past, present and future are all the same. When you think something in your conscious mind it sends the feeling to your subconscious, which then communicates to the Super Subconscious to create your thoughts. It takes what you are thinking and constructs them into your life experience and makes them physical. Understanding how the Super Subconscious works is vital in understanding such things as miracles, coincidences, and the laws of the universe. Some people call it God, Buddtha, Allah, or luck. Whatever you call it, it is real and it controls all!!!

Whether You Believe or Not the Laws Are Working!

The Universal Laws are working even if you don't know them or don't believe in them. The best tangible example of this is the law of gravity. If you throw something in the air it WILL come down. The law of gravity doesn't require your belief system in order to work... it just is! Similarly, the laws of the universe are what they are and are ALWAYS working. Every time we focus on something we are calling it towards us through our super subconscious mind. By using our thoughts and beliefs, we invite the people who are in our lives, the situations that shape our experiences and the material things that add or take away from our human existence. By nature we have EVERYTHING we need to manifest our dreams and we can do so instinctively but because of the noise in the outside world we often use our energy for resisting what we don't want instead of focusing on what we do want. This process is invoking one of the laws of the universe without us even being aware of it. That's why it's important that we understand how certain universal laws affect our lives so that we can use them in the right way .

If you simply did nothing but meditate and listened to your intuition then you would undoubtedly achieve all of your dreams but this still requires that you are in the right mindset. In order to deliberately manifest your dreams you need to have the proper perspective to recondition your Conscious and Subconscious mind so that the Super Subconscious can take over and make the miracles happen. Anyone who is wealthy has created a mindset of abundance that has allowed their Super Subconscious to take over and give them whatever they concentrate more on, which is abundance. Unfortunately, the same is true for those who are not wealthy; whether that's monetarily, spiritually, or in their relationships. Whether they know it or not their Super Subconscious is giving them exactly what they are concentrating on which is lack of wealth. Your Super Subconscious is like a genie in the bottle. Be careful what you wish for, because your wish is its command. By reconditioning the Conscious and Subconscious, you will affect the Super Subconscious effectively and begin to live the life of your dreams.

What You Should Always Keep in Mind

It's your outlook that matters the most! As the late Wayne Dyer would always say "If you change the way you look at things, the things you look at will change." It's never our situation that gets better or worse, it's the way we perceive the situation that brings on chaos or bliss. The world is the way we see it and it is our own mental attitude the makes the world what it is for us. Our thoughts make things beautiful or ugly, happy or sad, positive or negative...The whole world is in our own minds and we fully decide which world we want to see. It's like the parable of the two wolves. An old Cherokee is teaching his grandson about life. He says to the boy "A fight is going on inside me, it is a terrible fight and it is between two wolves. One is evil – he is anger, envy, sorrow, regret, greed, arrogance, self-pity, guilt, resentment, inferiority, lies, false pride, superiority, and ego." He continues, "The other is good – he is joy, peace, love, hope, serenity, humility, kindness, benevolence, empathy, generosity, truth, compassion, and faith. The same fight is going on inside you – and inside every other person, too." The grandson thinks for a minute and then asks his grandfather, "Which wolf will win?" The old Cherokee simply replied, "The one that you feed." This is not to say that unwanted things don't happen in life, but as they do happen it is your perspective that will dictate what happens next. Feed evil and negativity and that is EXACTLY what you will continue to experience. Feed goodness and optimism and your life will be bliss. Everything that happens in the world happens for a reason and regardless of the reason you must always realize that

Mind Right, Life Right

Life is Beautiful! The good, the bad, and the ugly are all working for your greater good.

This is why you should always stay in love.

Love your circumstance, love your struggle, love your life, love the people in your life, love the people around your life, love everything that you see, love everything that you experience. Just stay in love because love is the law of life! You cannot love yourself without loving everything that is you and since what you see or experience are things that are a part of you, then you must love it all. As you love it all this feeling and perspective will guide you towards the things that you really love which will help you manifest your dreams.

This is usually the hardest pill to swallow because most will ask "how can you love that which is undesirable?" And to that the answer is two fold. First it isn't about loving things that are undesirable, instead it is loving and accepting the fact that whatever is happening or has happened in your life had to happen in order to get you closer to your true desires. We doubt that the caterpillar wanted to go through the excruciating pain of breaking out of the chrysalis in order to become a butterfly but without this process there would be no way that the caterpillar can gain the strength in its wings that it needs to make the beautiful transition. Secondly, love is a natural healer. When you can express love for yourself and others, regardless of outside circumstances, this is bliss and this feeling of bliss will attract more abundance to you than you can even imagine. Staying in love brings you unconditional self-acceptance, deep self-awareness, and an unwavering appreciation for every moment of life. It allows anything that you are going through to become easier to deal with because of the attention and perspective that you have consciously decided to give to it. Without love we suffer and with this suffering we bring on feelings like depression, anxiety, anger, violence, and self-hatred which all moves us in the opposite direction of manifesting our dreams.

Life also serves as a mirror

As long as we live, life will teach us lessons, and the universe has a way of teaching us these lessons by making our outside world an exact reflection of our inner world. If you really want to know how you feel deep inside, take a look at your surroundings and what you are attracting. If you feel loved, safe, secure and happy inside, then you will have loving and happy people in your life that make you feel safe and secure. If you feel angry, self-critical or self-hatred, you will have people who get angry at you, or put you down or show hate towards you. The universe literally rearranges itself to reflect your reality. You cannot experience or be affected by that which is not a part of you. To that end, if what you are feeling is not what you want to feel, change what you see and that will begin the inner healing process.

It is also important that you stay organized in your life. It is said that when your environment is cluttered, the chaos will restrict your ability to stay focused and limit your brain's ability to process information as well as you would in an uncluttered, organized, and relaxing environment. This means that the reason why your perspective may be off is because of the chaos that you are seeing which continues to give you more of the same. Take a look at your home, closet, work space, and any area where you spend a lot of your time. Is it unorganized, cluttered, shabby or all of the above? Your home and work space are a true reflection of your head space.

Effective immediately, we must begin moving in the right direction by deliberately creating peace and harmony in our lives, in relationships, in how we see things, in what we experience and in what we put out to this world. This is the beginning of your best life where you are in control and become one with the universe to manifest all of your dreams and aspirations.

PART II

F@#K THE LAWS THAT GOVERN THE UNIVERSE

Mind Right, Life Right

The Never Ending Quest for Knowledge

Knowledge is a tricky thing; Erykah Badu once eloquently stated, "The man that knows something knows that he knows nothing at all." Which means that the more you seek out knowledge the more you'll realize that the knowledge you currently have is nothing compared to all of the information and wisdom that is out there in the world. To add to that, as stated in 1 Corinthians 8:2, "Those who think they know something, do not yet know as they ought to know." Or as Socrates puts it "A man who knows he knows nothing is smarter than a man who thinks he knows something but really knows nothing." This simply means that a true quest for knowledge is a never ending quest. There are no absolutes in the world, so to any conclusion that you may come up with, there will always be more information that either supports that conclusion, contradicts that conclusion, or makes that conclusion seem completely ridiculous. That's why there is so much separation in the world. Whether it's between religion and science, spirituality and the Bible, the Koran and the Tao Te Ching, The Old Testament vs the New Testament, Christianity vs Judaism vs Buddhism vs Islam vs Bahá'í Faith vs Hinduism or Taoism vs New Age Thinking... most people want certainty. There is a human desire to know what is right or wrong and the need to operate under that structure. There is also the need to know the outcome of the choices we make in life. Whether heaven or hell is in the afterlife or is it here on earth NOW? Is there truly only one life to live or do we keep coming back until we get it right? Has the outcome of our lives already been predestined or do we have free will to choose as we want? Is there a meaning to life or is this one big Matrix-like virtual simulation.

I've asked myself many of these questions and every time I did, I got a different answer. The more clarity I tried to obtain the more confused I became and that's because light can impair vision as much as darkness can if you're not ready for the light. Just as your eyes need time to adjust to light if it's been closed for too long, is how your mind must adjust to knowledge. Receiving too much information at once can cause an overload that creates confusion and hinders our ability to live. While searching for the answers to brighten our future we can potentially dim out the shine that exist today. That's why it's important to accept what feels right to you now and reject what feels wrong. Period! Not in the spirit of fighting against knowledge, but in the spirit of not forcing anything to make sense. In the spirit of going with the flow and knowing that what needs to be revealed to you will be revealed easily in due time. For this reason I say F@#k the Laws of the Universe! Not that they don't matter, just that if we focus too much on what they are and how we can manipulate them to our benefit, we can get stuck in a life of figuring things out instead of simply just living and manifesting our dreams!

As I said earlier, when the student is ready the teacher will appear. Life and lessons come to you in stages and as your consciousness increases you'll be ready to accept different truths. The aim should be to learn with an open heart, learn with no prejudgment, learn without making assumptions, learn without emotionally rejecting things before you fully compre-hend them. As you do this you will gain more under-standing on how the universe works and you will be guided intuitively. Your soul will awaken and lead you to your destiny.

Our True Purpose is to Find Our Purpose

No one truly knows why we are here but as we search for our reason, we become alive instead of just merely existing in a world that has been dictated to us based on someone else' desires. For thousands of years, we have been taught how to live by those who came before us. We were told about the consequences of not following the teachings that were left for us to follow. Many interpretations paint a picture of a vengeful and punitive God that will repay us for our wrong doings. What many fail to realize is that no matter what we believe in, every human being has been given free will by their higher power to do as they wish with their life. The universe doesn't tell us what we can or can't do, but instead gives us back exactly what we put out to the world through the law of Karma and the Law of Cause and Effect. We are 100% responsible for the consequences of our actions. Contrary to popular belief the Universe does not aim to punish us. The universe is here to assist us in manifesting whatever we decide to conjure up. If we ask for peace, love and happiness through our thoughts, intentions, and actions then that's what we will experience. If we ask to live in doom and gloom based on what we decide to keep our focus on, then that wish will be ours as well. We decide which direction our life goes. We live in a world that is created for us by us. Give love then get love, spread hate then hate will come back to you, live in fear and fear will be your companion. In fact for thousands of years, fear has been one of the biggest emotions that has held many back from living the lives that they truly deserve. Release the spirit of fear and live in love; as you live in love you begin to increase your level of consciousness, which will ultimately lead you to your destination. Keep in mind that the path to your divine self will not be a straight path. Sometimes it's easy to get lost in our physical form but as philosopher Pierre Teilhard de Chardin once said "We are not human beings having a spiritual experience. We are spiritual beings having a human experience." In order to evolve during our human experience it is necessary that we encounter duality on our journey. This is why we can recognize good and evil, light and darkness, happiness and sadness; these contrast or "the ying and the yang" as some call it, give us greater perspective and guides us toward our soul's desires. As Curtis Jackson once said "Joy wouldn't feel so good if it wasn't for pain." Knowing what you don't want is just as important as knowing what you do want.

Having duality coupled with the right to choose, allows us to act on free will in the world. This gives us the right to be the master of our fate and the co-creator of our world. To be clear, free will does not give anyone the right to violate anyone else's right to exist and act. As you will learn shortly, every action has a reaction, so while exercising your free will if you aim to undermine or deprive others of their free will then there will undoubtedly be consequences that you must deal with.

In this way, the universe gives us balance and adds order to what can easily become chaos. Manifesting our dreams is about following our souls desire and as we develop a higher level of consciousness our desires will undoubtedly change. Learning how to manifest our dreams is the fun part because as we recognize our power we come to grips with the fact that life is exactly what we make it. This is the Path of Self-realization.

PART III

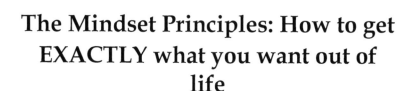

The Mindset Principles: How to get EXACTLY what you want out of life

Mindset Principle #1

Accept Your Divine

Right of Abundance

"The Universe is ready and willing to give you EVERYTHING your heart desires. Know and believe that abundance is your Birthright."

-Ash Cash (@IamAshCash)

Mind Right, Life Right

Many years ago, a young man and his family lived in the jungle and ruled over the lions. The lion as you know is usually the king of the jungle with access to just about anything it wants but for some strange reason this family was able to conquer the lions and become its masters.

As the young man became a teenager, everything he learned about the lion in school was being contradicted by what he saw in the jungle. One day he stopped, confused by the fact that the strong and ferocious lions were being held by only a small rope tied to their front leg. No chains, no cages, no special equipment; just a small rope. The family controlled everything about the lion, when it ate, when it played, when it could roam around. It was obvious that the lions could, at any time, break away from the ropes but for some reason, they did not.

One day the young man stopped one of his uncles and asked him why these strong animals just stood there and made no attempt to get away.

"Well," the uncle said, "when they were very young and much smaller we used the same size of rope to tie them and, at that age, it's enough to hold them. As they grew, they were conditioned to believe they cannot break away. They think the rope can still hold them, so they give up trying to escape long before they reach adulthood."

The young man was astonished. "You mean these animals could at any time break free from their bondage and reclaim their natural habitat, but because they believe they can not, they were stuck, held right where they were by one flimsy rope?" The uncle chuckled.

Just like the lion, many of us go through life hanging onto a belief that we cannot have or do something, simply because we have accepted a false reality that something is holding us back.

In order to begin to manifest our dreams, the first step is to realize that abundance is our birthright and everything in the universe is ours if we believe we can have it. Many of us have been conditioned to believe that there is lack and limits to what we can have and do. Do not let the conditioning and supposed limits dictate the outcome of your life! There is absolutely nothing you cannot do or have, if you put your mind to it.

At this very moment you have within you, everything you need in order to make your wildest dreams a reality but only if you choose to accept your divine birthright. We live in a Universe of abundance and the universe will ALWAYS give you what you believe. Believe in its abundance and it shall be yours, but believe in lack, then that is what you will experience. This is Spiritual Law.

The Law of Abundance is available for all of us to use, at all times. There are no conditions, there are no wrongs that we have to right. All we have to do is truly believe in the overflowing good that is available and we will receive and create it in our lives.

Now is the time to awaken our consciousness and recognize that there is enough in the world for all of us. There is enough light, love, compassion, food, wellness, money; you name it! There is always enough. ALWAYS!!!

Use the following affirmations as a tool to re-wire your abundant mindset. Use them daily if you must or as many times as needed, just remember that the conversations you have with yourself are the most important conversations that you can possibly have. You begin to believe what you tell yourself repeatedly.

Affirmations for an Abundant Mindset:

What I believe, I will receive. Abundance and prosperity is my birthright and I have it here and now!

I focus on abundance and prosperity and thereby attract it to me.

I allow all good things to come into my life and I enjoy them.

I let go of all resistance to prosperity and it comes to me naturally.

I am open to receiving an abundance of wealth, health, and happiness.

I always have what I need when I need it.

By appreciating what I already have, I manifest more abundance.

I love the exciting opportunities of wealth and abundance that come my way.

I am surrounded by people who are eager to contribute to my abundance.

I manifest abundance with my unique gifts and talents.

I create the exact lifestyle I want to live with enthusiasm.

I celebrate life, love, and abundance every day.

Mindset Principle #2

Be Intentional

"Your dreams will begin to manifest when you become intentional with your thoughts, feelings, and actions. The Universe responds better to purposeful intentions."

-Ash Cash (@IamAshCash)

Mind Right, Life Right

A couple were dining out together celebrating their 40th wedding anniversary. After the meal, the husband presented his wife romantically with a beautiful very old platinum antique locket on a chain. Amazingly when his wife opened the locket, a tiny fairy appeared.

Addressing the surprised couple, the fairy said, "Your forty years of dedication and loyalty to each other has released me from this locket, and in return I will now grant you both one wish each - anything you want..."

Without hesitating, the wife said, "My wish is to travel the world with my husband, as happy and in love as we've always been."

The fairy waved her wand with a flourish, and magically there on the table were two first-class round-trip tickets to all of the beautiful countries around the world.

Deeply shocked, the couple looked at each other, unable to believe their luck.

"Your turn," said the fairy and the wife to the husband.

The husband thought for a few seconds, and then

said, with a little guilt in his voice, "Forgive me, but to really enjoy this gift of a lifetime, traveling around the world - I yearn for a younger woman - so I wish that my wife could be thirty years younger than me."

Shocked, the fairy glanced at the wife, and with a knowing look in her eye, waved her wand...

and the husband became ninety-three.

The Law of Intention works EXACTLY in this way. You can have anything you want but it is important that you are clear about your wishes and understand that the universe will never impose ill-will on someone else in order to manifest your dream.

Being clear means that any thought that is held with purposeful intention will manifest itself. The intended thought, can also be in words but must be followed by your actions. You can't say you want your dream then not follow through with what it takes to obtain it. By doing this the Universe is unclear about what your true intentions are; it doesn't know what you want because you are thinking and saying one thing but doing another.

Manifesting your dreams is never an accident, doesn't happen by coincidence, and will never be about luck or about what cards you are dealt! To truly make your dreams a reality you have to be intentional with your actions! Period!

Are you doing what needs to be done to be a success or a failure? Your actions or lack thereof will be the main thing that seals your fate!

The Universe doesn't care about what you're about to do. You are either doing it or not! Someone who intends to be great isn't on that path unless they are **DOING** what it takes to get there! Imagine you intend to win a championship but never go to practice! Imagine you intend to take a flight out of the country and never buy a ticket! Or what if you intend to live a healthier lifestyle but never exercise or eat right! My point is that if you want to make your dreams a reality, you must stop intending to do it and simply go out and do what has to be done!

Your dreams are yours for the taking... the only thing you need to do is make the decision that you are going to take it! This will require time, persistent, commitment, patience, and wisdom but if and when you stay focused you will be astonished by how everything you want becomes your reality.

Now is the time to begin to be thankful for your

dream before it has manifested. You must feel confident in its attainment and never second guest whether it will happen. It is not a question of IF but WHEN!

How you feel plays a major role in manifesting your dreams. The more positive emotions you have for your dreams and aspirations, the quicker they will manifest. But I must stress your subsequent actions matter just as much. Without actions to support your thoughts and emotions, your desires will have a hard time manifesting into your life.

Also, because we live in a world with many distractions, it can become difficult to stay focused, that's why it is important that you create a ritual that will keep your dreams in your mind's eye. One ritual that is very effective is daily affirmations of your definite chief aim. Begin by writing down ALL of your deep desires in the affirmative using I AM. For example, if your desire is to be a millionaire then you will write "I AM a Millionaire." If your desire is to run a successful business then you will write "I AM a successful business owner who...." Now, read your affirmations every day and night until it becomes part of your belief system and it allows you to be intentional with your actions. (TIP: Add them as a daily calendar reminder on your smart phone or tablet to assure you never miss a day).

Mind Right, Life Right

Affirmations for Purposeful Intentions:

I empower my dream by directing all of my thoughts and actions towards its manifestation.

I transform my thoughts into reality by taking positive action.

By taking positive actions, I bring more positive results into my life.

I am ready to do whatever it takes to make my dream a reality.

I demonstrate my commitment through the actions I take.

I am grounded in the experience of the present moment.

With laser-focus, I know exactly what needs to be done and I do it.

I am committed to putting 100% effort into my goals.

Today, I abandon my old habits and take up new, more positive ones.

I act on all inspirations as they are received.

I am completely dedicated to doing everything it takes to reach my highest potential.

My daily positive actions move me closer and closer to my dream.

Mindset Principle #3 - ALWAYS look on the bright side

"The Universe will ALWAYS give you what you put your focus on! Change your perspective and see the good in ALL situations."

-Ash Cash (@IamAshCash)

Mind Right, Life Right

One day a psychology professor entered the classroom and asked his students to prepare for a surprise test. Baffled by this, the students waited anxiously at their desks for the test to begin. The professor handed out the question paper, with the text facing down as usual. Once he handed them all out, he asked his students to turn the page and begin. To everyone's surprise, there were no questions just a black dot in the center of the page. The professor seeing the expression on everyone's face said to the students, "I want you to write down what you see."

The students confused, got started on the seemingly unchallenging task. At the end of the class, the professor took all the papers and started reading each one of them aloud in front of all the students. All of them with no exceptions, described the black dot, trying to explain its position in the middle of the sheet, how large it was, what it may have represented, etc. After the professor read all of the papers, he began to explain:

"I am not going to grade you on this, but you all failed miserably! No one wrote about the other part of the paper. Everyone focused on the black dot – and the same happens in our lives. We have a blank piece of paper to observe, enjoy, and do what we please with, but we always focus on the dark spots."

This is an example of how we push aside and delay our dreams from manifesting. There will always be reasons to celebrate life but instead of using our time wisely to show gratitude for all that we have, we use it to remember the dark spots!

We focus on the health issues that bother us, the lack of money, the complicated relationships, the disappointment with a friend, the things we should've done and where we should've been by now, etc.

The blank piece of paper represents the fresh start that we all have access to that allows us to rewrite our today the way we want it to be and the dark spots are not even a fraction of the possibilities, but unfortunately that's what consumes our mind.

If we only stop for a second to realize that as we enjoy and appreciate all of our blessings, it is only then that we fully experience life and have access to all of our dreams and aspirations. The more we remember the dark spots or use a negative experience from our past to dictate our future, the further away we push our dreams from manifesting.

The Law of Attraction shows us that we create the things, events, and people that come in and out of our lives. Our thoughts, feelings, words, and actions produce energies that attract like energies. Negative attracts negative and positive attracts positive. You attract what you are and what you concentrate most on.

Simply put, where your attention goes, your energy flows. Focusing on the negative will indeed produce more negative, so it is imperative that if you want your dreams to manifest themselves then you have to focus on the positive. Always look on the bright-side!

Life can be miserable or life can be a happy adventure. It's all on how you view it! Oftentimes, we believe our circumstances dictate how well our lives will be but our attitude is the real dictator of our circumstance! Those who can see the bright side in ANY situation are those who are destined to live their best life possible! On the other hand, those who whine, complain, or have a victim mentality are unfortunately destined for doom and gloom!

Understand that how you view something is how it will manifest! You know the saying… You can complain that roses have thorns or be happy that thorns have roses! Either way, your disposition is in your control and will dictate how life will develop!

This reminds me of a story I heard about an old

billionaire shoemaker who had no next of kin and wanted to step down and leave his fortune to someone. Because he had no successor he decided that he would choose one of his top salesmen.

He pulled both in a room and asked them to travel to a certain part of Africa to investigate and report back on market potential.

The first salesman reported, "There is no potential here - no one wears shoes!" The second salesman reported back, "There is massive potential here – no one wears shoes!" The billionaire shoemaker left his fortune and business control to the second salesmen.

In this example and in life, it is looking at the brightside that will help you manifest your dreams. No matter what is happening there is ALWAYS a positive outlook that will help you in your journey.

Everything in the Universe is just energy manifested into physical or non-physical form, the positive energy that you put out in ALL situations can attract and manifest your dreams into your reality.

Mind Right, Life Right

<u>Affirmations for a Positive Mental Attitude:</u>

I accept only positive thoughts, feelings and actions.

I think positively no matter what.

Positive thinking is transforming my life.

I always choose positive thoughts over negative thoughts.

I use the power of positive thinking to reach my goals.

All my thoughts are positive and empowering.

I always find the positive in everything.

I think positive thoughts and radiate positive energy with ease.

I think positively even in difficult or stressful situations.

I find it easy to have positive thoughts at will.

Positive thinking is a natural part of who I am.

Because I am a positive person, I attract positive and empowering people into my life.

Each and every day, I reprogram my mind to focus on the positive in everything.

I focus on the positive, I know my life is unfolding as I desire.

Each positive thought I have has taken me one step closer to my dream.

Mindset Principle #4 - Accept What Is and Change What You Can

"What you resist will persist. Never fight against the undesirable. Change what's in your power to change and accept what you cannot."

- Ash Cash (@IamAshCash)

Mind Right, Life Right

One day a farmer was walking his two donkey's down an old path in his farm and of no fault of their own, they both fell down into two separate wells. The animals cried sadly for hours as the farmer tried to figure out what to do. Finally he decided that the animals were too old and not worth saving, and that the well needed to be covered anyway. So he invited all his neighbors to come over and help him.

They all grabbed a shovel and began to shovel dirt into the first well. The first donkey began to cry loudly!! The cries became louder and louder as it realized what was happening. All he could think of was how loyal he had been to the farmer and was distraught that his owner didn't do more to save him. As he whined and cried pitifully in his mind he pleaded for everyone to stop throwing dirt on him. Eventually the cries subdued and the donkey was buried alive in the hole.

The second donkey met a different fate however. As the farmer and the neighbors began to shovel dirt on him at first he cried horribly. Then, to everyone's amazement, he quieted down. A few shovel loads later, everyone looked puzzed and decided to look down the well to see what was happening and was astonished at what they saw. With every shovel of dirt that hit his back, the donkey was doing something amazing. He would shake it off and take a step up. As the farmer's neighbors continued to shovel dirt on top of the animal, he would shake it off and take a step up. Pretty soon, the donkey stepped up over the edge of the well and trotted off to everyone's amazement.

In life, many people will throw dirt on you and try to bury you for no good reason. Many circumstances and obstacles will come your way that will seem to be life shattering and like you have no control over. The key to getting over these circumstances is to accept what is and change what you can.

In the first instance, the donkey was so focused on his terrible circumstance that it didn't rely on its own power to survive and thrive. It used all of its energy to whine and complain instead of doing what it could do to save itself. The second donkey, focused on the problem in the beginning but eventually realized that if he were to survive he needed to use the dirt that was being thrown on him to his advantage.

Focusing on what you have the power to change will always lead you down the path of manifesting your dreams. The Law of Resistance tell us that what we resist will continue to persist. The more we fight against something the more we are drawing it to us.

Mind Right, Life Right

Resistance stems from fear, so as we let go of what we are afraid of, we are subconsciously calling to us more of what we do want. This doesn't mean to ignore your fears as if they don't exist, instead it means to face them until they no longer have an effect on you.

When we use words like don't, can't, won't or not, we are calling to us the very thing that we are speaking against. This may seem illogical but the truth of the matter is that our conscious mind has the ability to discern between a negative and a positive instruction. Our subconscious mind, on the other hand, cannot tell the difference.

Whenever we say "We don't want to lose, we can't keep going through this, we won't stay in the same place, or we will never do so and so" it may seem as if these are positive thoughts moving us in the right direction but in fact we are calling upon us the very experience that will keep those situations at bay. Instead we need to focus on winning, on the situations we want to see, on the places we would rather be, etc.; Instead of resisting failure or poverty we must attract success and wealth, instead of not wanting to be lonely, we should focus on the love we want. It's never in our best interest to go against anything. It is imperative that we embrace the positive, rather than resist the negative.

In the same breathe it is important to pay attention to what we are resisting. Anything that we are against has a message for us. If we continue to see the same patterns of failure, we need to come to grips with what part of success makes us afraid. We hold on because we are afraid to lose. Fear is the biggest emotion that holds us back from manifesting our dreams. The faster we face our fears, the sooner our dreams become a reality. This is done by learning to use conscious detachment.

The Law of Conscious Detachment says that when we accept what is, we accept the unalterable realities in our life without resisting them. This means that you should allow any undesirable experience in your life that you cannot change flow through you without resisting it and without allowing it to affect your state of being. By doing this your ability to live the life you deserve becomes a reality. This concept is not about just letting go but about trusting and believing that all things are working for your good. It is about allowing yourself to focus your energies on the things that you can change in order to create your bliss, which is the state of being that we want to be in, to attract the favorable circumstances that will allow our dreams to come to fruition.

Some things are what they are and no matter how

much we resist them, there is nothing that can be done about them. It will never serve you positively to waste energy on any level trying to change what you cannot change.

As the famous serenity prayer says "God grant me the serenity to accept the things I cannot change; courage to change the things I can; and wisdom to know the difference." Or as the Buddhist teachings tell us, "It is our resistance to what is that causes our suffering."

If we want to do away with money hardships, relationship problems, loneliness, sickness, guilt, unfulfilled desires, etc. then we must be committed to detachment.

This includes detaching ourselves from people and how we expect them to behave. Instead of holding onto your idea of how things should be, allow yourself and those around you the freedom to be as they may. Detach yourself from certainties and allow yourself to be OK with uncertainty. In fact, allow uncertainty to be part of your experience without holding onto any preconceived notions.

Become excited about the infinite possibilities that exist in the universe and know that everything happens for a reason so as you continue to journey towards manifesting your dreams, accepting what is and changing what you can will keep you open to infinite choices.

Mind Right, Life Right

Affirmations for Accepting What Is:

I accept and release everything in my life that is beyond my power to change.

I accept and appreciate the reality I have created for myself.

I take full responsibility for making the most of my life.

I am totally at peace with my past.

I accept life without judgment or criticism.

I unconditionally accept everyone I meet as they are.

I accept myself completely and unconditionally.

I accept that all things are possible with intent and belief.

I see the world through eyes of love and acceptance.

I acknowledge and accept endless possibilities for my life.

I allow my mind to accept and enjoy all that is good and positive in my life.

I trust the flow and processes of my life.

I willingly let go of trying to control every tiny detail, and let peace and acceptance guide my life.

I relax and allow the universe to give me what I want and need.

Mindset Principle #5 - Only Take Actions That Support Your Desires

"Every action has an equal or greater reaction, therefore it is imperative that you only engage in actions that brings you closer to your dreams."

–Ash Cash (@IamAshCash)

Mind Right, Life Right

There once was a lady who had the desire to be rich since she was a young girl. She thought that she would work thirty years and after she retired her riches would appear. During her retirement she realized that she would have to go about being rich another way.

One night as she watched the evening news, she saw a couple win the lottery and while collecting their check they thanked God. She immediately thought to herself surely the lottery was the way she was going to get rich, so she got on her knees and prayed to God that she would win.

Every night, she got down on her knees and pleaded with the Almighty to hit the jackpot. After a week, she noticed that she hadn't won so she traveled to Ireland to get a four-leaf clover. She went to a ranch and bought a horseshoe, then traveled to a rabbit farm to obtain a rabbit foot. Still no luck, she waited for a shining star and wished to the universe that she would finally win.

After a month and still no fortune, she looked to the heavens and wondered why God still hadn't granted her prayer.

One night she heard a loud booming voice come

from above that simply said, "At the very least you could have bought a lottery ticket!"

This funny but accurate anecdote portrays how many of us l treat our higher power. We wish and pray for things and everything but what it takes to make those things become a reality.

We involve ourselves in busy work but don't realize that any action that doesn't feed our dreams is action that takes away from it. Thoughts without action is a daydream, just like faith without works is dead. In fact, "Faith without proper work is dream suicide!"

The Law of Action must be applied in order for us to manifest our dreams and aspirations. This means that we cannot simply just ask for our dreams with our words and feelings, we must engage in actions that support our thoughts, emotions and words so that our dreams can become a reality.

Every action has a reaction or consequence, so nothing in the universe happens by chance or by coincidence. You do nothing, you get nothing. You do a lot, you get a lot! You do a lot towards nothing, you get a lot of nothing! It is a simple universal law equation: You will ALWAYS get out of life what you put in to it. This Universal Law of Cause and Effect is always working and applies to the blessings and abundance that are readily available to us.

NOTHING you do will ever be in vein. This is why massive action towards your goal will ALWAYS manifest your dreams! (Maybe not exactly when you want it, but we'll talk about that later).

With the proper use of this law you can change any condition in your life. To put it another way, the law of cause and effect states that every effect has a specific and predictable cause, while every cause or action has a specific and predictable effect. This means that everything that we currently have or experience in our lives is an effect that happened because of a specific cause. There are no accidents, chance, luck, or coincidences!

The decisions we make and the actions we take on a daily basis is the cause for everything in our lives. ALL DECISIONS MATTER!! It doesn't matter if it's a "small" and "insignificant" decision or a seemingly "big" or "life transforming" decision, every single decision we have ever made and action we have ever taken has set into motion a series of events that have created predictable and specific effects that we are now experiencing in our lives.

We once believed that if we changed our thoughts we can change our circumstance but in fact, if we change our thoughts AND subsequent actions, we change our circumstance.

Manifesting your dreams and achieving success in any part of your life is predictable and can be repeated if you stay present in the moment and conscious of what you are doing. When you make the right decisions, and take the right actions then you will without a shadow of a doubt, manifest all of your dreams and aspirations!

Mind Right, Life Right

Affirmations for Taking Action:

All my actions support my dreams.

All of my actions reflect my intentions.

By taking positive actions, I bring more positive results into my life.

Every action I take moves me closer to my goal.

Every activity I perform is in accordance with the commitment to my goals.

Everything I do supports my desires for the future.

Everything I do takes me closer to my dreams.

I act on all inspirations as they are received.

I am committed to putting 100% effort into my goals.

I am completely dedicated to doing everything it takes to reach my highest potential.

I demonstrate my commitment through the actions I take.

I eagerly anticipate the positive outcomes of the actions I take every day.

I empower my dream by directing all my thoughts and actions towards its manifestation.

I pledge to take action towards my goals every day.

I relentlessly work towards my dream.

Mindset Principle #6 - Embrace Your Struggles

"Adversity exist only to strengthen where you are weak. When you successfully overcome obstacles you are signaling to the universe that you are ready for the next level of life."

-Ash Cash (@IamAshCash)

Mind Right, Life Right

A young woman one day went to her mother to complain about how hard life was for her. She was at her wits end and was ready to give up. She was tired of fighting and struggling. It seemed as if when one problem was solved, a new one turned up. Her mother took her to the kitchen and filled three pots with water, placing each on a high flame. Soon the pots started to boil.

In the first she placed carrots, in the second she placed eggs, and in the last she placed ground coffee beans. She let them sit and boil, without saying a word.

In about twenty minutes she turned off the burners. She took the carrots out and placed them in a bowl. She pulled the eggs out and placed them in a bowl. Then she poured the coffee out and placed it in a bowl. Turning to her daughter, she asked, "Tell me what you see."

"Carrots, eggs, and coffee," she sarcastically replied.

Her mother brought her closer and asked her to feel the carrots. She did and noticed that they were soft. The mother then asked the daughter to take an egg and break it. After pulling off the shell, she observed the hard-boiled egg. Finally, the mother asked the daughter to sip the coffee. The daughter smiled as she smelled it's rich aroma. The daughter then asked, "What does it all mean?"

Her mother explained that each of these objects had faced the same adversity boiling water and each object reacted differently.

The carrot went in strong, hard, and unrelenting. However, after being subjected to the boiling water, it softened and became weak.

The egg had been fragile. Its thin outer shell had protected its liquid interior, but after sitting through the boiling water, its inside became hardened.

The ground coffee beans were unique, however. Instead of allowing the boiling water change them, they changed the water.

"Which are you?" she asked her daughter. "When adversity knocks on your door, how do you respond? Are you a carrot, an egg or a coffee bean?"

In this story, the carrot starts off strong, but with pain and adversity it softens and loses all of its strength. The eggs starts with a flexible and kind heart, but allows the heat to change it. The shell may look the same, but on the inside it is tough and bitter!

The coffee bean becomes one with the hot water, the very circumstance that was supposed to bring it pain. When the water got hot, it released its fragrance and flavor changing the composition of the hot water. What started out as a trial and tribulation became a favorable situation that allowed the coffee bean to maximize its full potential. In fact, without the hot water, the coffee bean would have just merely existed never knowing how awesome and flavorful it could become.

Be like the coffee bean! Understand that struggle is part of the journey! What you go through on your way to manifesting your dreams is just as important as the dream itself! NEVER for one second take your struggles for granted! Embrace them, love them, and use them to get the life you deserve! As the saying goes "You have to fight through some bad days to earn the best days of your life."

The Law of Relativity tells us that everyone will receive a series of problems (Tests of Initiation) for the purpose of strengthening the light within. If we pass the test/solve the problem, we will then be given access to our dreams and aspirations. When those tests come, we have to view them in the proper light and stay connected to our hearts in order to be successful.

This is why it is imperative for us to embrace our struggles instead of fighting against them or wishing they didn't exist. The pursuit of our dreams is like a video game; the closer you get to your destination the harder the game becomes! You can either be satisfied with getting past the easy levels or you can continue to move forward until you master the game and get what you came for. Victory is ALWAYS just one step past your greatest defeat, so if you ever feel that you are at your wits end just hold on a little longer and your desires shall be yours.

The Law of Relativity also teaches us to compare our problems to others' problems and put everything into its proper perspective. How can we complain about not having new shoes when someone doesn't have feet? No matter how bad we think our situation is, there is always someone who is in a worse position. It is all relative. This shouldn't be done in the vein of complacency nor in a way that makes you feel guilty for pursing your dream. It should be done as a way to keep you focused on your dream so that you can have the proper energy and mindset to turn them into reality. Why wake up stressing, when all of life is a blessing? Keeping this in mind will help you on your journey so that you can put problems in their proper place.

Mind Right, Life Right

As stated earlier, there are no accidents, chance, luck, or coincidences, so everything that you have experienced or are experiencing has/is happening for a reason. Sometimes that reason is to teach us a lesson that will make us stronger. There are no mistakes ever in life, only lessons. So as tempting as it may be to look back in regret over decisions that you "should've" or "could've" made, know that you are EXACTLY where you belong and that what you went through was a piece of the puzzle that was needed to get you to where your heart wants to go.

Growth is a process of trial and error and since hindsight is always 20/20 you won't know what part of the process your problems serve until you continue to push past them to reach your goals.

Keep in mind that you can never escape a lesson or overlook what life is trying to teach you. A lesson will be repeated over and over until it is learned. It may be presented to you in different forms but at the core it is the same situation. When you have complete- ly learned a lesson, you will then go on to the next one.

Learning lessons does not end. In fact, this is what life is about, learning and growing. When you stop growing then you are dead! (literally and figuratively).

It is also important to note that the universe will never give you more than you can handle, so no matter what you go through know that you already have everything you need to overcome any obstacle and learn any lesson. There is nothing you have to do first, life is and will always be what you make it.

Your experience is neither good nor bad, it is neutral. You decide what value you want to place on whatever you are going through. You determine what way you want to experience your situation. The hopes is that you choose to experience it in such a way that you learn whatever lesson life is trying to teach you so you can move closer to manifesting your dream and living in bliss.

Regardless of what you decided, the Universe will ALWAYS support your choice, and bring you whatever you need to live out your experience in the way that you intended. The good news is that at any time you can make a different choice and go in a different direction. As John Lennon once famously said "Everything will be okay in the end. If it's not okay, it's not the end." Embrace your struggles and learn life's lessons!

Mind Right, Life Right

Affirmations for Overcoming Obstacles:

I make the best of every situation.

I am open to looking at my problems from a new perspective.

I know that challenges are not only inevitable, but an important part of life.

My job is to stay focused and be ever watchful for the wisdom the universe provides.

I always find a way to overcome life's obstacles.

I see the hidden lessons in all problems that arise in my life.

I am grateful for what life's problems teach me.

Challenges stimulate and inspire me.

There is no problem in my life that cannot be solved with a fresh perspective.

I confront and conquer all obstacles in my way.

I am purposefully dismantling all barriers to achieving my goals.

I use obstacles as stepping stones to success.

I transform problems into unique opportunities for growth.

Mindset Principle #7 - Understand the Power of Collaboration

"No two like-minds can come together without creating a third and more powerful like-mind. Use the power of collaboration to manifest your dreams faster."

–Ash Cash (@IamAshCash)

Mind Right, Life Right

There is an African proverb that states "If you want to go fast, go alone. If you want to go far, go together." Geese know this saying all too well. As each goose flaps its wings, it creates an 'uplift' for the birds that follow.

By flying in a "V" formation, the whole flock adds about 71% greater flying range than if each bird flew alone. When a goose falls out of formation, it suddenly feels the drag and resistance of flying alone. It quickly moves back into formation to take advantage of the lifting power of the bird immediately in front of it.

When the lead goose tires, it rotates back into the formation and another goose flies to the point position. The geese flying in formation honk to encourage those up front to keep going! When a goose gets sick, wounded or shot down, two geese drop out of formation and follow it down to help protect it. They stay with it until it dies or is able to fly again. Then, they launch out with another formation of geese and try to catch up with the flock.

There are multiple lessons that can be learned by the way geese move to accomplish their goals. First, geese show us that if you connect with people who share a common goal and sense of direction, you can get where you are going quicker and easier because you are traveling on the collective power of one another.

Second, success leaves clues; If you are with a group that is vibrating on your same wave length then it is in your best interest to follow the lead.

Third, when you share resources, knowledge, life experiences, and take turns sharing leadership, then you can accomplish way more together than you could ever accomplish alone.

Fourth, We need to make sure that we are part of a positive and encouraging group that helps motivate each other to keep pushing forward towards our dreams. Where there is encouragement, there is a greater likelihood of the attainment of ALL dreams and aspirations.

Lastly, a group that is truly on the same wave will understand that not all days are alike and that there will be times that extra support is needed. In these times the group will stand by each other. With the right group there is cohesion during difficult times as well as when things are all good.

In universal law terms, this is what we call the Law of Collaboration or The Power of the Mastermind.

Mind Right, Life Right

When two or more people of similar vibration are gathered for a shared purpose, their combined energy, when focused on that purpose is doubled, tripled, quadrupled or more.

This concept of the Mastermind alliance has been around for years and has been used by everyone from ancient Kings and Queens to Hip-Hop artist and entertainers. Many entrepreneurs and business owners use it today to increase their level of success exponentially. It was first introduced to the masses by Napoleon Hill in the classic book, "Think And Grow Rich," it describes the process of combining like minds in order to create a greater force. Hill defines it as "The coordination of knowledge and effort of two or more people, who work toward a definite purpose, in the spirit of harmony."

Forming a Mastermind group is imperative in your quest for manifesting your dreams. Each person serves as an accountability partner for one another. They challenge each other to set powerful goals, and push each other to accomplish them. Masterminding is about commitment, confidentiality, willingness to give and receive advice and ideas, and the support of one another with total honesty, respect and compassion. Spending time with this person/group will undoubtedly move you closer to ALL of your dreams and aspirations.

Under spiritual law, once you find your tribe, if you want help, you must ask for it. It is better to help another only when they ask you for help. Giving or getting the wrong type of help can be detrimental to achieving ones dreams and aspirations. It's similar to the story of the man and the butterfly, A man spent hours watching a butterfly struggling to emerge from its cocoon. It managed to make a small hole, but its body was too large to get through it. After a long struggle, it appeared to be exhausted and remained absolutely still. The man decided to help the butterfly and, with a pair of scissors, he cut open the cocoon, thus releasing the butterfly. However, the butterfly's body was very small and wrinkled and its wings were all crumpled. The man continued to watch, hoping that, at any moment, the butterfly would open its wings and fly away. Nothing happened; in fact, the butterfly spent the rest of its brief life dragging around its shrunken body and shriveled wings, incapable of flight.

What the man – out of kindness and his eagerness to help – had failed to understand was that the tight cocoon and the efforts that the butterfly had to make to squeeze out of that tiny hole is nature's way of training the butterfly and strengthening its wings.

Mind Right, Life Right

This is a great example of how the wrong kind of help can actually hurt someone. Sometimes, it is that little extra effort and struggle that prepares us for the next obstacle to be faced. Not being allowed to go through certain struggles can leave one unprepared to fight the next battle and like the butterfly, they never manage to fly off to their destiny.

As stated before, struggle is part of the journey! What you go through on your way to success is as important as the success itself!

This doesn't mean that you should struggle just for the sake of struggling. There are times when you may wish to ask for help. This should be done calmly and with strength. Your state of being when requesting help is important as well, remember: What you resist will persist!

Whether it is from your mastermind group or through other sources always remember that as soon as you are ready to ask for help you are also ready to receive it. Just the thought and action of asking for help indicates that you are ready to accept the wisdom that goes with it.

The universe is always working for your greater good so it will align all of the resources that you need to give you the assistance that you requested. When you need help first quiet and center yourself. Meditate on what you really want and find clarity about it. Remember that the universe is abundant so don't limit your request. The universe is waiting to help you. All you have to do is ask.

Mind Right, Life Right

Affirmations for Successful Masterminds:

I understand the power of collaboration. I attract like-minded people into my life.

I am the average of the five people I spend the most time with, so I choose my friends wisely.

I am open to receiving true and reliable guidance in marvelous, unexpected ways.

I get all the help and support I need.

All of my friendships are meaningful and rewarding.

I have deep connections with the people I choose to interact with.

I only develop relationships with positive, uplifting people.

I attract positive, passionate people into my life.

My friends empower and inspire me.

Because I love who I am, I naturally attract positive relationships into my life.

My circle of influence continues to grow beyond what I ever expected.

I choose healthy relationships based on mutual love and support.

There is an abundance of support for me in the Universe.

Mindset Principle #8 - Give What You Want to Get Back

"You will undoubtedly reap what you sow. Only put out in the world that in which you are willing to get back and that which will lead you towards your desires."

-Ash Cash (@IamAshCash)

Mind Right, Life Right

An old carpenter was ready to retire. He had worked more than 30 years for the same company and proudly never had one recall on his workmanship. He told his boss of his plans to leave the house building business and live a more simple and relaxed life with his wife enjoying his extended family.

He would definitely miss the money and the camaraderie he had with his team but he knew he was making the right decision. The boss was sorry to see such a dedicated and skilled employee go and asked if he could build just one more house as a personal favor. The carpenter said yes, but in time it was easy to see that his heart was not in his work. He resorted to shoddy workmanship and used inferior materials, covering his mistakes over so they weren't obvious. It was an unfortunate way to end his career.

When the carpenter finished his work and the builder came to inspect the house, the boss handed the front door key to him. "This is your house," he said, "my gift to you for all your hard work, dedication, perfectionism and honesty."

For 30 years this carpenter did great work and as a result he had a great career, surrounded by great people and received great compensation. But when he grew weary and began to feel unappreciated, taken advantage of, and decided to not move with integrity, this backfired on him and created a situation where he blocked his blessing.

By now you know that like energy attracts more like energy, which is an important part of the law of attraction but as it relates to manifesting your dreams it goes deeper. The Law of Tenfold Return is a universal law that says that whatever you give, whether it's money, time, donations, deeds or anything else within your life, you will receive the same back multiplied 10 times. This includes love, kindness, compassion, etc.

The more that you give the faster it will multiply. But you cannot trick the universe. Giving simply for the sake of receiving will not net you anything because your intention is really to take from the universe, so it will give you nothing as a way to take from you. Remember, you get what you give or as the famous bible scripture says "Be not deceived; God is not mocked; for whatever a man soweth, that shall he also reap."

To truly activate this law, all of your giving MUST be done in love! Anything that you do that comes from the heart WILL be returned and multiplied tenfold! Give with the love and joy and feel the energy of the giving. Believe in the abundance of the universe and know that there will NEVER be lack!

Mind Right, Life Right

You must be grateful in advance for your tenfold return, at the time you are sowing your seed. It's truly like planting; when you put a seed into the ground, even though you don't see what's happening underneath the dirt, you know that with time and proper care that small seed will sprout to a beautiful plant with benefits way beyond the original seed.

Your thoughts, emotions, and the act of giving is the process of planting your seed within the universe. Only putting out with love that which you want to receive is the care and love needed to begin the process of letting your dreams sprout.

This law is irrefutable and works every time. The only way you can fail is if you quit sowing with love! As in the example with the carpenter, he negated his tenfold return because he started to sow negative seeds of resentment, dishonesty, and selfishness.

Love is the secret ingredient, so make sure that if you heart isn't in something that you don't involve yourself. The carpenter could have simply declined doing the work and his blessings would have stayed intact because of the seeds he had sown prior. He agreed to give in love but his actions were the opposite and this is what caused the issue. Your intentions are important. Never make a commitment that you don't intend on keeping.

It is also very important that you understand that you must give before you can receive, but conversely, you must also receive in order to give. This is the part of manifesting our dreams that many people overlook. When we truly understand the law of tenfold return we realize that as we allow pride, ego, and/or arrogance to stop us from taking from those who are giving with love, we block their blessings as well as ours. Energy flows in a circular motion so there has to be a cycle of good created, to complete the law and make it effective.

Believe that what you sow you shall reap, but also as you reap you must continue to sow. Be blessed to be a blessing to others so you can continue the cycle of good. Have faith in this concept, and know without a shadow of a doubt that this principle will work for you. Your blessing may not come from where or who you may expect them to come from, but just know that they are coming. Set your intention and know that they will. Focus your mind and visualize what you really want and leave the details to the Universe.

One last thing, ALWAYS show gratitude for all that you receive. No matter how big or small, give thanks for ALL of your blessings.

Affirmations for Good Karma

What I give out returns to me.

I freely give out of abundance that is within me.

I am a loving, generous, and kind person.

The more I love, the more that love is returned to me.

As I give, I freely receive the universal abundance.

I give and receive with joy.

I am a magnificent being with an abundance of power and love to give

Everything I give to others is a gift to myself. As I give, I receive.

Miracles are a natural part of living and giving.

I give and receive freely, generously, with open heart and open mind.

Mindset Principle #9 - Allow Your Desires to Come to Fruition

"You must have unwavering faith in the abundance of the universe and know without a shadow of a doubt that ALL of your desires WILL become reality in divine time."

-Ash Cash (@IamAshCash)

Mind Right, Life Right

Years ago in Scotland, the Clark family had a dream. Clark and his wife worked and saved, making plans for their nine children and themselves to travel to the United States. It had taken years, but they had finally saved enough money and had gotten passports and made reservations for the whole family on a new liner to the United States.

The entire family was filled with anticipation and excitement about their new life. However, seven days before their departure, the youngest son was bitten by a dog. The doctor sewed up the boy but hung a yellow sheet on the Clarks' front door. Because of the possibility of rabies, they were being quarantined for fourteen days.

The family's dreams were shattered. They would not be able to make the trip to America as they had planned. The father, filled with disappointment and anger, stomped to the dock to watch the ship leave - without the Clark family. The father shed tears of disappointment and cursed both his son and God for their misfortune.

Five days later, the tragic news spread throughout Scotland - the mighty Titanic had sunk taking hundreds of lives. The Clark family was to have been on that ship, but because the son had been bitten by a dog, they were left behind in Scotland.

When Mr. Clark heard the news, he hugged his son and thanked him for saving the family. He thanked God for saving their lives and turning what he had felt was a tragedy into a blessing.

Years later the Clark family finally achieved their dream of coming to America, where they started a few family businesses and thrived!

This story has so many messages tied into one. The main message is something that a close friend of mine always says, "Rejection is protection!" Many times on our road to manifesting our dreams, we get to a point where we are very close to its attainment, then something happens that seems to be setting us back. What we need to realize is that all setbacks are a setup for a comeback. Not now is not no! A delay in the manifesting of your dream can very well be the universe protecting you from something that you cannot see or don't know about.

The Universe is ALWAYS at your service so when you ask for something, it will conspire to give you EXACTLY what you want. Many times we want to control or receive our dream in a certain way not realizing that it is our limiting belief that tells us that there's only a few specific ways that we could attain it. The universe has unlimited access to every possible way that you can manifest your dream, you just have to believe and relinquish control!

Your dream will materialize in divine time. There is no need to be impatient, no need to force the issue, and no need to begin to doubt whether you will receive it. It is actually these emotions (doubt, impatience, anxiety) that delay the attainment of our dreams.

Patience is defined as the capacity to accept or tolerate delay, trouble, or suffering without getting angry or upset. This is literally how the Law of Allowance works. The Law of Allowance is the law that basically allows our dreams to manifest through our thoughts, words, and deeds. It is the process of focusing on what we want, holding the desired experience in our minds eye, feeling good about its attainment, envisioning its outcome, and allowing it to manifest with full faith.

It may sound simple but The Law of Allowance is one of the hardest to practice because it needs interaction between both, the Law of Attraction and the Law of Intention. As we think about our desires and work towards making them a reality, we also subconsciously put time limits on when we want them to happen (which is usually immediately). If our dreams don't materialize when we want them to, doubt starts to creep in and we grow impatient.

The truth of the matter is that it is hard to have total faith on something that we cannot see, especially when we are fighting against external influences and trying to let go of old thought processes. Because the Law of Allowance is hard to practice, it is also the law that gives you the greatest opportunity for manifesting your dreams; this is why it is the final step in getting exactly what you want. Once you master this step, you will be astonished at how fast you begin to manifest your desires.

The key to its mastery is either using focusing techniques to keep your desires front and center in your mind's eye or forgetting about your desires temporarily through what I like to call the Law of Distraction!

Both ways are effective but it really depends on you! The key is that you don't want to force focusing techniques or you don't want to distract yourself so much that you shift your energy to asking the universe for something totally different.

Focusing techniques include affirmations, vision boards, listening to success stories, reading self-help books, etc. You have EVERYTHING you need to manifest ALL of your dreams and aspirations so these techniques truly don't have any power in and of themselves. We don't need to do them, but because some of us may have limiting beliefs, fears, negative viewpoints of the world, or limited positive influences, focusing techniques can play an important role to keep us on track during our journey to manifest our dreams. They allow us to focus our energy in a positive way so that our emotions can lead us to the manifestation of our desires, instead of shifting our energy negatively being impatient or disappointed. Your feelings are what are most important you attract what you feel!

That's why focusing techniques don't always work. For some people, saying affirmations, reading positive quotes, or looking at a vision board can perpetuate bad feelings especially when someone is feeling irritated, dispirited, depressed, or feeling like they are sick of the work they are doing. In these moments, you want to practice the Law of Distraction.

The Law of Distraction is the process of doing something that has no direct correlation to your dream or aspiration but raises your vibration and makes you feel good. This can be playing your favorite sport, hanging out with your best friend, watching a comedy that makes you laugh, etc. The goal is to distract yourself from thinking about your dreams but raising your vibration to a positive level that opens the door for manifestation. The universe doesn't forget what you wished for so the act of feeling good will continue to flow good things in your life, including what you desire.

Allow your dreams to manifest! Have total faith in your higher power and know that everything is working on your behalf, so even if you don't understand why certain circumstances are taking place, know that it is all leading to what you have asked for. The question should never be IF your dreams will materialize, but WHEN! Let the universe do what it does and live in bliss!

Affirmations for Allowing Dreams to Manifest

I deserve to have a great life.

I deserve to manifest ALL of my dreams and aspirations.

I allow my mind to accept and enjoy all that is good and positive in my life.

My good comes to me from every direction.

I am open to receive!

I deserve, and accept all of the goodness this world grants me daily.

With patience and optimism, I achieve all that I desire.

I know that patience is more than just waiting... it is persisting.

I have unwavering faith that all of my dreams will come to fruition in divine time.

I believe that I have the right to live the life I desire.

I am fully deserving of abundance, happiness and blessings.

PART IV

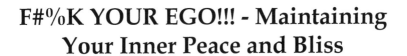

F#%K YOUR EGO!!! - Maintaining Your Inner Peace and Bliss

Mind Right, Life Right

Now that we know how to manifest our dreams and aspirations it is time to talk about how we maintain our inner peace and bliss. Imagine there was this thing that existed, that you never seen before but it had total control over your life!

It told you how to feel, how to act, and how to respond to things. It gave you direction on how to react to criticism and how to perceive praise. It made you believe that what you have or what you do was the definition of who you really were.

It gave you the perception that there was a right or wrong way to live and that anyone who didn't conform to this norm was responsible for the current state of affairs in the world. It made you believe that the way people treated you or reacted towards you had a direct correlation to who you were.

This thing controlled your emotions and went from one extreme to the next. From feelings of self-deprecation that causes you to belittle yourself, diminish your light, and undervalue yourself, to those that are self-destructive which give you the audacity to sabotage your success, punish yourself or do harm to yourself.

This thing gives you emotions that make it ok for you to deny full responsibility for yourself. It can make you stubborn and stuck in your ways, giving you the false rationale for resisting change in your life. This thing fuels greed, selfish overindulgence, over-consumption and arrogance.

It can make you impatient, uncompassionate, intolerant, and easily frustrated. This thing that I speak of is none other than your EGO. No one has ever seen it, yet it's power and control is undeniable.

As we begin to manifest our dreams, the EGO is the one thing that can single handedly stop us from living in bliss. Our EGO is an illusion despite how influential and convincing it can be. Many of us allow our EGO to make us believe that it is who we really are when in fact our true-self is waiting patiently ready to allow our soul to experience harmony. Our EGO makes us too dependent on the outside world instead of a natural dependency on our innate self.

This EGO-illusion and false perception can literally kill us inside. It's like the parable of the dog in the castle...

Once upon a time a king built his beautiful dream castle that had all its doors and walls made of mirrors.

Mind Right, Life Right

One night, before anyone occupied this beautiful work of art, a homeless dog walked in looking for shelter.

Instead of seeing the beauty of the castle, the first thing that the dog saw was hundreds of other dogs looking back at him from the mirrors. To protect himself from what he perceived as danger, the dog bared its teeth aggressively, indicating hostility and that it was ready to fight. Subsequently all of the other dogs bared their teeth. The dog became cautious and began to growl but the only thing that the dog heard was a loud growling echo; this castle had excellent acoustics.

The dog became scared and realized that its life was in danger and so the dog began to bark as loud as it could to defend itself. The louder the dog barked the louder he heard the echo of hundreds of dogs.

The next morning, when people came into the castle, they found the homeless dog lying there dead. Obviously, the dog didn't die because somebody killed it, but instead it died because it fought its own reflection. It tried to protect itself from hundreds of reflections of itself that really posed no harm.

This is how the EGO operates; it amplifies all which is around us and kills every opportunity that we have to live in peace. It sends us false messages about our true nature and leads us to make assumptions about the world around us. It takes everything personal, makes everything about it and gives us this false sense of self-importance and self-absorption. Every time we take offense to something that someone says or does it is our EGO guiding that thought.

In addition, when we think we are better or smarter than someone it is our EGO in operation. When we think to ourselves "it is not my fault" or "He or she should've done this or that," it is this type of egocentric thinking that stands in the way and hold us back from finding love, peace, bliss and ultimately manifesting our dreams.

This is why it is imperative that we banish our EGO. If we really want to maintain peace and bliss we must understand that we are one with the world. Removing your ego gives you the power to truly control your life. It's what allows YOU to finally take full responsibility for YOUR actions, and remove the blame we often want to place on others. Taking back control of your life from your EGO will allow you to maintain your peace and bliss. In addition to that, the following 10 steps will also add harmony to your life:

Mind Right, Life Right

1. <u>Stay in Your Lane</u>

Your life is your life and where you decide to walk will determine how far you go! While on your journey to greatness you will always see other journeys and struggles that look similar to yours! You will be tempted to follow what worked or didn't work for others! You will rationalize your action or lack thereof based on other people's experiences and create your facts solely on how closely other people's paths resemble! This may be the biggest mistake that you can ever make! I don't care how similar a path may look or how closely tied two goals may be; only you can create your own path! What works for one may not necessarily work for the other! What's good for the Goose isn't always good for the Gander!! Stop allowing other people to dictate where you go and how you get there! This is your life and the lessons in it are yours to learn! Don't be afraid to blaze your own trail and shine your own light! Your greatness in life is undeniable! As long as you have the courage to go wherever your heart leads you then you will have satisfaction to enjoy whatever your heart desires!! Stay in YOUR Lane!!! Your treasure is at the end of the tunnel!

2. Go With Your Flow

Life is as easy as you allow it to be! The answers to life's questions and what you ought to be doing are answered always through how you feel! Your gut feeling, intuition, and heart will guide you and tell you when you are going in the right direction! Go against it and you will never find happiness! No matter how hard you try, it is impossible to fit a square in a circle and vice versa! Trying to force things to go a certain way is fighting against the flow of life! The Good, The Bad, and The Ugly all have their purpose! Don't fight it! Don't question why! Just understand that everything has its place and every experience is a life lesson! As you continue your journey in this game we call life, remember that you are exactly where you are supposed to be! Go with the flow and allow life to guide you! Your happiness depends on it!!

3. Clean Up Your Circle

Relationships MUST be mutual. The word literally means the way in which two or more concepts, objects, or people are connected, or the state of being connected which means that somehow you must relate. Most of the time, because of past history, a false sense of loyalty, or other ridiculous reasons, we find ourselves holding on to relationships that are no longer mutually beneficial! We carry on this dead weight then wonder why we are having difficulties climbing mountains. It is imperative that we associate ourselves with only positive, focused people who we can learn from and who will not drain our valuable energy with uninspiring attitudes. You must make sure everybody in your boat is rowing & not poking holes while you're not looking. Get to know your circle then make adjustments as necessary. Always remember only a knife can sharpen a knife! Stay on your level and build yourself higher!

4. Be Better, Not Perfect

Some of us go through life afraid to make mistakes! Some of us try at all costs to cover up what went wrong as if we're supposed to be perfect! The biggest mistake a person can make is to not accept mistakes for what they really are which are opportunities to get it right! Life is a continual learning process! It doesn't matter if you're 15, 50, or 90. There is something that you will learn every single day that you are on this earth! The most important part of this learning process is what you learn from your mistakes!! These lessons will absolutely become the catalyst for your greatness!

The more mistakes that are made the faster you will realize what not to do! If you stay focused sooner or later you will run out of mistakes and the only thing that is going to be left is the way to your bliss"! Don't give up your opportunity to be great by trying to be something you're not! Perfection should never be your goal but being the best that you can possibly be will get you close! Be Better, Not Perfect! Keep Learning! Keep Making Mistakes! Keep Learning from those mistakes and never ever give up! The world and everything in it is yours! Keep your eyes on the prize!!

5. Write Your Own Rules

Imagine being given a blank sheet of paper and being told that no matter what happened in the past, no matter what your beginnings where, and no matter where you are today, this sheet of paper can be used to write down how the rest of your life will look? How creative would you be? How triumphant would this story end? Would you be a hero or a villain? Would you write it as a love story, an inspirational story, or a tragedy? Hopefully whatever you choose is what you really want in life and you realize that this is exactly what TODAY brings! Each day gives you the opportunity to write the perfect story because you are the author of your own life. Unfortunately many people believe you are writing in pen and can't erase your mistakes but best believe that if you are intentional about where you want to go, your future will be better than your past! It is up to you to figure out whether you will continue to be a victim of circumstance or if you will use your past struggles and obstacles to move you to the next level of life! You need to start recognizing the truth of your story, then finish the story. Whatever happened, happened! But you're still here, still capable, and powerful beyond belief! You are not your circumstance! It happened and you made it through. You are still more than fully equipped with every single tool you need to fulfill your purpose! You can either make it happen or make excuses you can't do both! Nothing Can Stop You But YOU and it's Always Too Early To Quit!!! Learn to embrace these facts and write the most compelling life story that will live on even after you are gone! You are in total control! Take the power and make your life great!

6. <u>Go Dumb!</u>

There are many people who live within the limitations of what reality says is possible. There are also people who can only see within the four walls in the box that society has given them. There are people who will fight tooth and nail to maintain this way of life… Then there are the delusional, the insane, the misguided who think that they can accomplish things that have never been done! These ridiculous people have this notion that if they just believe in the unseen it will somehow just appear! These wackos try to defy everything that conventional wisdom has ever tried to teach them….. But truth be told this second group of rule breakers are the innovators, the creators, the people who move our world forward! So who are you? Do you live in a box or are you insane? Will you keep the world the way you found it or will you contribute something great to it? Remember that anything is possible. Whatever the mind can conceive is real and can happen. Don't get trapped in a mental prison that just gives you below the minimum that life can offer. Understand that believing in the unseen is the only way to make it happen. Create a new reality, one that defies the norm and pushes your creativity to the limit! It is all possible! Be ridiculous and make the impossible happen!

7. <u>Live in the Moment!</u>

It is estimated that 150,000 people die worldwide each day. That's 150,000 people who no longer can take a breathe. 150,000 people who can no longer dream and 150,000 people who have no more chances to take. As you read these words realize that tomorrow is not promised! As your eyes scroll further understand that when your time is up your time is up. But also realize that your moment is NOW. There's nothing to wait for simply use what you have at this very moment to create your happiness! Yesterday doesn't want you and tomorrow is running from you. This is your moment. Live in it. Cherish it and make it great! Take NOW for granted if you want but NOW has been the only time that has ever consistently been by your side. Show your appreciation and seize the Moment! You only have one live to live!! Live it NOW! Live it right!!

8. <u>Stay Blessed and Highly Favored!!</u> –

Joel Olsteen once said "One of the main reasons that we lose our enthusiasm in life is because we become ungrateful; we let what was once a miracle become common to us. We get so accustomed to our blessings that it becomes a routine and we devalue it.." Make sure that on your road to greatness that you don't take for granted all of the advantages that you already have in your corner! Realize that the mere fact that you are still alive means that your life still has purpose. Right now as we speak your life is exactly where it needs to be; all of your experiences have brought you exactly to this place and what you do with it RIGHT NOW will determine how high you continue to go! Stop being ungrateful and appreciate where you are and where you are about to go!

9. <u>Don't Think About It Too Much!!</u>

Albert Einstein once said "The intuitive mind is a sacred gift and the rational mind is a faithful servant. We have created a society that honors the servant and has forgotten the gift." In ALL situations you already know instinctively which is the right way to go but because we allow our inner voice to get drowned out by the outside world we second-guess ourselves and cause unnecessary pain and suffering. If you really paid attention, you would know right from the beginning what was for you and what wasn't. In most cases, our initial intuitive response is the best indicator of how things will turn out later. If you listen to the voice and don't talk yourself out of it for one reason or another, you will begin to travel on the path towards your ultimate happiness and success! Don't think about it too much! You heart will NEVER let you suffer if you are in search of your dreams. Some decisions may seem difficult to make but as you contemplate and procrastinate you are digging yourself deep in a hole. If the gut says to do it... then just do it! Trust your intuition and live the life you deserve!

10. <u>Stay Committed ALWAYS!!</u>

They say commitment means staying loyal to what you said you were going to do long after the mood you said it in has left. Many times we make the grave mistake of being satisfied with our intentions. We think that because we intend to do something that it is enough to help us actually attain it. While intent reveals your desires, only action can reveal your commitment. The fact of the matter is that if you truly believe something you will attempt to live it.... Not "I'm going to try it out"... Not "Let's see what happens"... Not "If circumstances permit".... But an unwavering commitment to make it happen no matter what! If the latter isn't your thinking than you need to recheck your commitment and belief level! Let today be the day that you become committed to being your dreams and aspirations! Let today be the day you commit to doing what it takes to make your dreams come true. Let today be the day you vow to get, achieve, and experience the life of your dreams!

PART V

CONTINUED READING TO ELEVATE YOUR MIND

As I mentioned earlier most of my knowledge comes from my experience plus from the many books that I've had the pleasure and honor of reading. The following are the top 13 books that are in my yearly rotation. I enjoy reading new literature but these are permanent mainstays that help renew and remind (See what I did there)

A Course in Miracles

A Course in Miracles is a classic in modern spirituality. The landmark guide is in as much demand today as it was when it was first published in 1975. This updated text is split into three volumes which include the text, workbook for students and manual for teachers. Although the course is Christian in statement, it deals with universal spiritual themes, and is designed to help achieve dramatic, lasting results in every aspect of your life.

The Alchemist, by Paulo Coelho

Paulo Coelho's enchanting novel has inspired a devoted following around the world. This story, dazzling in its powerful simplicity and inspiring wisdom, is about an Andalusian shepherd boy named Santiago who travels from his homeland in Spain to the Egyptian desert in search of a treasure buried in the Pyramids. Along the way he meets a Gypsy woman, a man who calls himself king, and an alchemist, all of whom point Santiago in the direction of his quest. No one knows what the treasure is, or if Santiago will be able to surmount the obstacles along the way. But what starts out as a journey to find worldly goods turns into a discovery of the treasure found within. Lush, evocative, and deeply humane, the story of Santiago is an eternal testament to the transforming power of our dreams and the importance of listening to our hearts.

A Return to Love: Reflections on the Principles of "A Course in Miracles" by Marianne Williamson

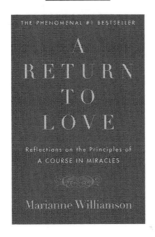

Marianne Williamson shares her reflections on A Course in Miracles and her insights on the application of love in the search for inner peace. Williamson reveals how we each can become a miracle worker by accepting God and by the expression of love in our daily lives. Whether psychic pain is in the area of relationships, career, or health, she shows us how love is a potent force, the key to inner peace, and how by practicing love we can make our own lives more fulfilling while creating a more peaceful and loving world for our children.

Manifesting Change: It Couldn't Be Easier by Mike Dooley

Author and international speaker Mike Dooley illuminates exactly how to move beyond the law of attraction to the next level—manifestation. In his most powerful and comprehensive work to date, Dooley reveals his master guide for following your heart and taking action on your dreams.

Manifesting Change explains the actual mechanics behind every dream, how you fit into the equation of "Reality Creation," and which steps you can take that will lead you to the desired end results without worrying about the details. Dooley expands upon the universal mysteries of why you are here, who you really are, and all that you deserve. It includes easy-to-understand exercises, stories, and analogies and reveals the extraordinarily unique concept, the "Matrix," that clearly shows the flow of events that will, or will not, automatically trigger changes in your life based upon your thoughts, words, and actions.

Manifesting Change is designed to slip past defenses and into the heart, and plant seeds that will blossom into understanding, action, and life changes.

<u>*Change Your Thoughts, Change Your Life by Dr. Wayne W. Dyer*</u>

Five hundred years before the birth of Jesus, a God-realized being named Lao-tzu in ancient China dictated 81 verses, which are regarded by many as the ultimate commentary on the nature of our existence. The classic text of these 81 verses, called the Tao Te Ching or the Great Way, offers advice and guidance that is balanced, moral, spiritual, and always concerned with working for the good.

In this book, Dr. Wayne W. Dyer has reviewed hundreds of translations of the Tao Te Ching and has written 81 distinct essays on how to apply the ancient wisdom of Lao-tzu to today's modern world. This work contains the entire 81 verses of the Tao, compiled from Wayne's researching of 10 of the most well-respected translations of text that have survived for more than 25 centuries. Each chapter is designed for actually living the Tao or the Great Way today. Some of the chapter titles are "Living with Flexibility," "Living Without Enemies," and "Living by Letting Go." Each of the 81 brief chapters focuses on living the Tao and concludes with a section called "Doing the Tao Now."

Ask and It Is Given by Esther Hicks

Ask and It Is Given, by Esther and Jerry Hicks, which presents the teachings of the nonphysical entity Abraham, will help you learn how to manifest your desires so that you're living the joyous and fulfilling life you deserve. As you read, you'll come to understand how your relationships, health issues, finances, career concerns, and more are influenced by the Universal laws that govern your time/space reality - and you'll discover powerful processes that will help you go with the positive flow of life. It's your birthright to live a life filled with everything that is good-and this book will show you how to make it so in every way!

Celestine's Prophecy by James Redfield

You have never read a book like this before -- a book that comes along once in a lifetime to change lives forever. In the rain forests of Peru, an ancient manuscript has been discovered. Within its pages are 9 key insights into life itself -- insights each human being is predicted to grasp sequentially; one insight, then another, as we move toward a completely spiritual culture on Earth. Drawing on ancient wisdom, it tells you how to make connections among the events happening in your life right now and lets you see what is going to happen to you in the years to come. The story it tells is a gripping one of adventure and discovery, but it is also a guidebook that has the power to crystallize your perceptions of why you are where you are in life and to direct your steps with a new energy and optimism as you head into tomorrow.

The Power of Now By Eckhart Tolle

It's no wonder that The Power of Now has sold over 2 million copies worldwide and has been translated into over 30 foreign languages. Much more than simple principles and platitudes, the book takes readers on an inspiring spiritual journey to find their true and deepest self and reach the ultimate in personal growth and spirituality: the discovery of truth and light.

In the first chapter, Tolle introduces readers to enlightenment and its natural enemy, the mind. He awakens readers to their role as a creator of pain and shows them how to have a pain-free identity by living fully in the present. The journey is thrilling, and along the way, the author shows how to connect to the indestructible essence of our Being, "the eternal, ever-present One Life beyond the myriad forms of life that are subject to birth and death."

Featuring a new preface by the author, this paperback shows that only after regaining awareness of Being, liberated from Mind and intensely in the Now, is there Enlightenment.

The Four Agreements: A Practical Guide to Personal Freedom (A Toltec Wisdom Book) By Don Miguel Ruiz

In The Four Agreements, bestselling author don Miguel Ruiz reveals the source of self-limiting beliefs that rob us of joy and create needless suffering. Based on ancient Toltec wisdom, The Four Agreements offer a powerful code of conduct that can rapidly transform our lives to a new experience of freedom, true happiness, and love.

The Seven Spiritual Laws of Success by Deepak Chopra

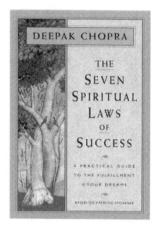

The creation of wealth has always been regarded as a process that requires hard work and luck--often at the expense of others. In this remarkable book, the author of Quantum Healing and other bestsellers reveals how to align with the subtle yet powerful, unseen forces that affect the flow of money in our lives.

<u>Conversations with God: Book 1, By Neale Donald Walsch</u>

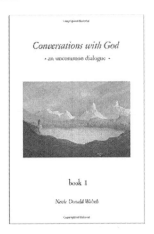

Conversations with God Book 1 began a series that has been changing millions of lives for more than ten years. Finally, the bestselling series is now a movie, starring Henry Czerny (The Pink Panther and Clear and Present Danger) and Ingrid Boulting (The Last Tycoon). Produced and directed by Stephen Simon (producer of Somewhere in Time and What Dreams May Come) and distributed by Samuel Goldwyn Films and Fox Home Entertainment, the theatrical release is set for October 27, 2006. The movie is the true account of Walsch (played by Cierny), who went from an unemployed homeless man to an "accidental spiritual messenger" and author of the bestselling book

The Seat of the Soul by Gary Zukav

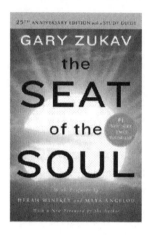

 With lucidity and elegance, Gary Zukav explains that we are evolving from a species that pursues power based upon the perceptions of the five senses -- external power -- into a species that pursues authentic power -- power that is based upon the perceptions and values of the spirit. He shows how the pursuit of external power has produced our survival-of-the-fittest understanding of evolution, generated conflict between lovers, communities, and superpowers, and brought us to the edge of destruction.

 Using his scientist's eye and philosopher's heart, Zukav shows how infusing the activities of life with reverence, compassion, and trust makes them come alive with meaning and purpose. He illustrates how the emerging values of the spirit are changing marriages into spiritual partnerships, psychology into spiritual psychology, and transforming our everyday lives. The Seat of the Soul describes the remarkable journey to the spirit that each of us is on.

<u>A New Earth By Eckhart Tolle</u>

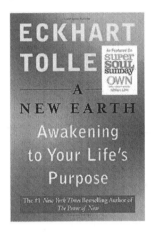

With his bestselling spiritual guide The Power of Now, Eckhart Tolle inspired millions of readers to discover the freedom and joy of a life lived "in the now." In A New Earth, Tolle expands on these powerful ideas to show how transcending our ego-based state of consciousness is not only essential to personal happiness, but also the key to ending conflict and suffering throughout the world. Tolle describes how our attachment to the ego creates the dysfunction that leads to anger, jealousy, and unhappiness, and shows readers how to awaken to a new state of consciousness and follow the path to a truly fulfilling existence.

Illuminating, enlightening, and uplifting, A New Earth is a profoundly spiritual manifesto for a better way of life—and for building a better world.

ABOUT THE AUTHOR

Ash Exantus aka Ash Cash is a speaker, bestselling author, business consultant, and spiritual adviser to entrepreneurs, celebrities, athletes, executives and high net-worth individuals.

If you are interested in purchasing bulk orders of any of the above books please call 917.740.2274 or email info@IamAshCash.com

For those of you interested in the possibility of Life or Business Coaching From Ash, contact him though his website www.IamAshCash.com

Mind Right, Money Right: 10 Laws of Financial Freedom, is a book designed to teach you how to effectively manage your personal finances. It shows you how having the right mental attitude and with laser sharp focus, you can have anything you desire in life. It's an easy to read book that anyone, at any level, can understand. The book's aim is to teach you these 10 proven Laws of Financial Freedom using the stories of wealthy men and women who have used them. This book is especially geared towards anyone who is tired of having a dependency on money and is ready to take some practical steps in order to correct it. Money is power but knowing how to make it work for you

is freedom; Mind Right, Money Right will teach you
how.

Have you ever spent time observing a child or
group of children and how they conduct their young
lives? The one thing you will immediately notice is
that they live life by their instincts. They are enthu-
siastic, always eager to learn, curious, brave, and
will try almost anything without hesitation. These
characteristics and more are all the keys to happiness
but unfortunately as we transition from childhood to
adulthood we replace these natural instincts with what
adults call "reality." As I watched my daughter Taylor
grow, I began to realize that she had not been tainted
by our ideas of "reality" and as a result was always
happy and tended to get everything she wanted out
of life effortlessly. Isn't that what we all want of our

lives? In the following pages you will read in detail the valuable lessons I've learned from my three year old daughter. Each chapter illustrates through the eyes of a child how you can live a happier life the way it was intended for you to live! Life is abundant! Life is enjoyable! Life is exactly how you imagined it in your wildest dreams! Today is the day that you bring it back to that essence!

Ask Ash Cash Volume 1 is a DVD series of questions by everyday people wanting to gain financial advice. With more than 14 years of banking under his belt, Ash'Cash is on a mission to financial re-educate every spectrum of humanity

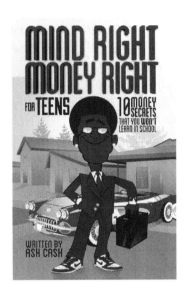

Mind Right Money Right for Teens, is the newest book in Ash'Cash's bestselling series about how to properly manage and grow your money by having the right thought process. This book doesn't just give you money secrets that will change your
life now but the lessons in this book will help change your life forever and give you the financial freedom you deserve. Based on the story of a young millionaire name Ben Frank, this book will show you:

- How to use your confidence to get anything you want in life.
- How to get rich by saving and investing your money wisely.
-Why its important to work to learn, not to earn.

-And why giving up is not always a bad thing.

Made in the USA
Middletown, DE
17 May 2020